Chariot Victor Publishing
Cook Communications, Colorado Springs, CO 80918
Cook Communications, Paris, Ontario
Kingsway Communications, Eastbourne, England

BLESSINGS AND PRAYERS FOR YOU

Design: Bill Gray, Cheryl Ogletree
Editor: Julie Smith

First printing, 1999
Printed in Singapore
1 2 3 4 5 6 7 8 9 10 Printing/Year 03 02 01 00 99

Library of Congress Cataloging-in-Publication Data
Blaylock, Carolyn
    Blessings and prayers for you/by Carolyn Blaylock
      p. cm.
    ISBN 1-56476-770-1
    1. Prayers. I. Title
BV245.B575   1999
242'.8--DC21

98-42206
CIP

Given with hugs in my heart

To

Lilyana McFarland

From

Sis Arlene Bright

On

Sept 30, 2018

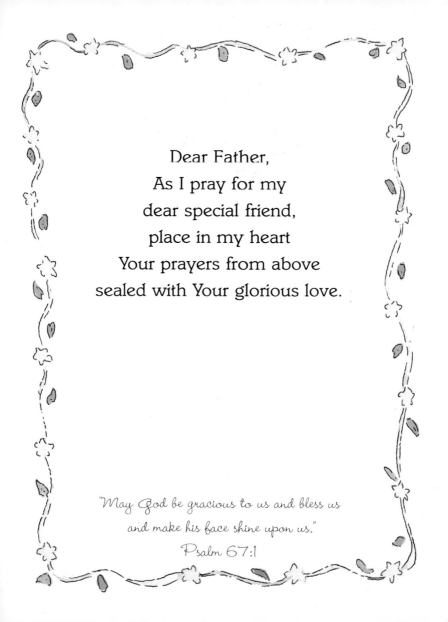

Dear Father,
As I pray for my
dear special friend,
place in my heart
Your prayers from above
sealed with Your glorious love.

"May God be gracious to us and bless us
and make his face shine upon us."
Psalm 67:1

You, my friend, belong to the Gardener of life

Lord, what a beautiful rose
You've made in my friend.
She carries Your fragrance,
unfolding the petals
of Your love
more and more each day.
Thank You for placing her
in the garden of my life.

"He has made everything beautiful . . ."
Ecclesiastes 3:11

May you awaken with whispers of sundrops across your face...

©Carolyn Blaylock

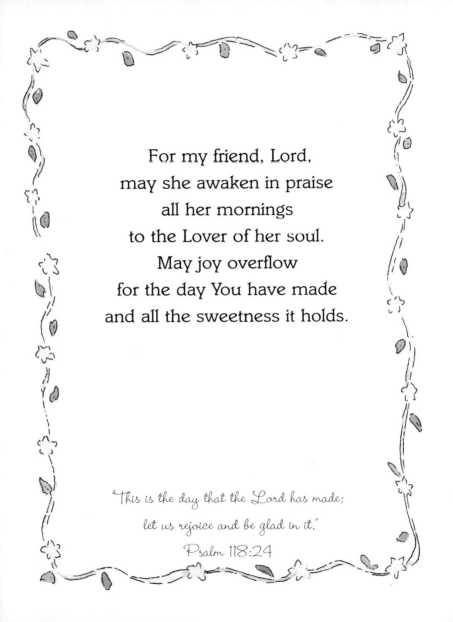

For my friend, Lord,
may she awaken in praise
all her mornings
to the Lover of her soul.
May joy overflow
for the day You have made
and all the sweetness it holds.

"This is the day that the Lord has made;

let us rejoice and be glad in it."

Psalm 118:24

Whatever is true... pure... lovely...

Think on these.

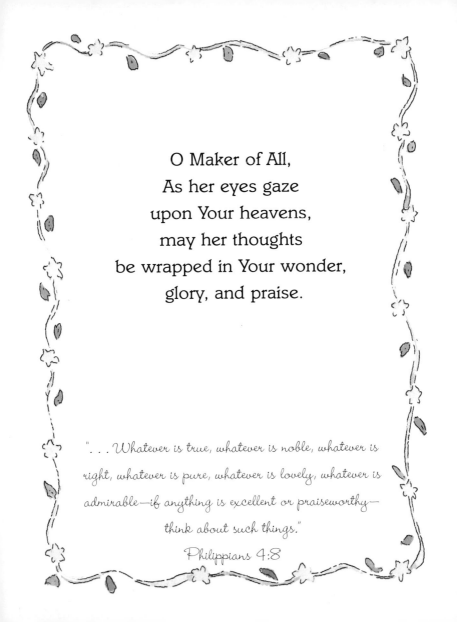

O Maker of All,
As her eyes gaze
upon Your heavens,
may her thoughts
be wrapped in Your wonder,
glory, and praise.

". . . Whatever is true, whatever is noble, whatever is
right, whatever is pure, whatever is lovely, whatever is
admirable—if anything is excellent or praiseworthy—
think about such things."

Philippians 4:8

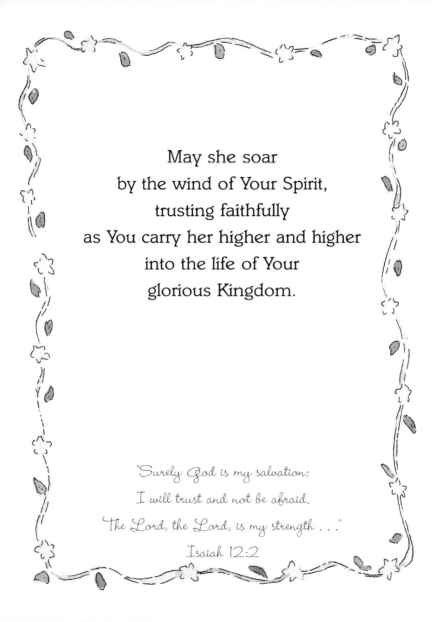

May she soar
by the wind of Your Spirit,
trusting faithfully
as You carry her higher and higher
into the life of Your
glorious Kingdom.

"Surely God is my salvation;
I will trust and not be afraid.
The Lord, the Lord, is my strength . . ."

Isaiah 12:2

Carolyn Blaylock©

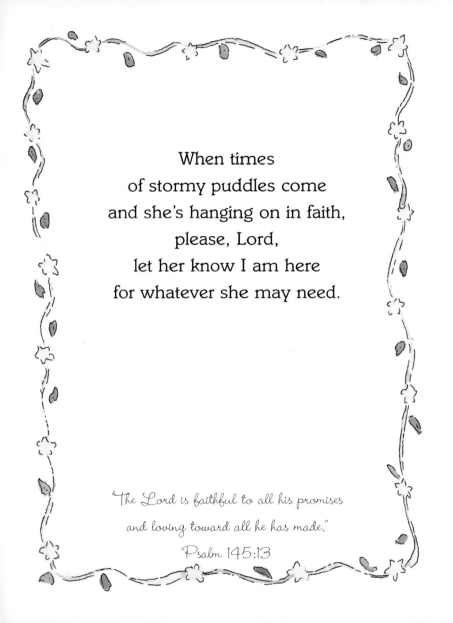

When times
of stormy puddles come
and she's hanging on in faith,
please, Lord,
let her know I am here
for whatever she may need.

The Lord is faithful to all his promises
and loving toward all he has made."
Psalm 145:13

Café a la Friend

whisper...whisper...
talk...talk...talk...
yakkity...yak...yak...

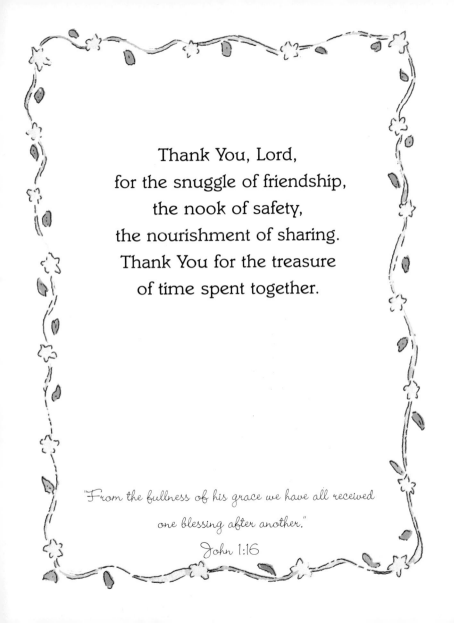

Thank You, Lord,
for the snuggle of friendship,
the nook of safety,
the nourishment of sharing.
Thank You for the treasure
of time spent together.

"From the fullness of his grace we have all received
one blessing after another."

John 1:16

You've
placed a smile
on so many faces.

©carolyn blaylock

Oh, how special she is,
placing smiles
on so many hearts.
Bless her as
she blesses others
with laughter, light, and love.

"You have put gladness in my heart."

Psalm 4:7 (NKJV)

Carolyn Blaylock ©

On tippytoes with outstretched arms,
my friend loves You so.
Please embrace her with
streams of Your light,
warming her heart and soul.

". . . The glory of the Lord is streaming from you."
Isaiah 60:1 (TLB)

Carolyn Blaylock ©

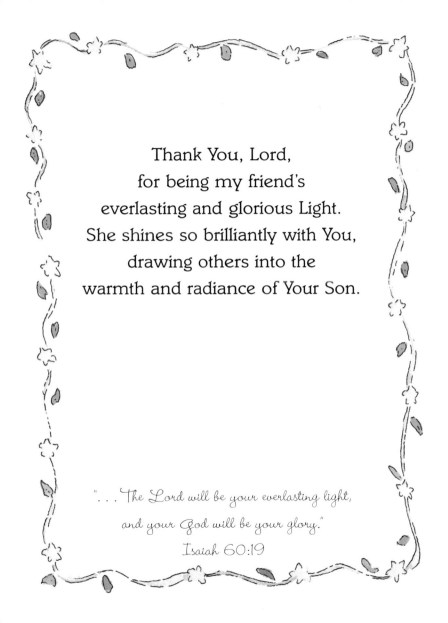

Thank You, Lord,
for being my friend's
everlasting and glorious Light.
She shines so brilliantly with You,
drawing others into the
warmth and radiance of Your Son.

"... The Lord will be your everlasting light,
and your God will be your glory."
Isaiah 60:19

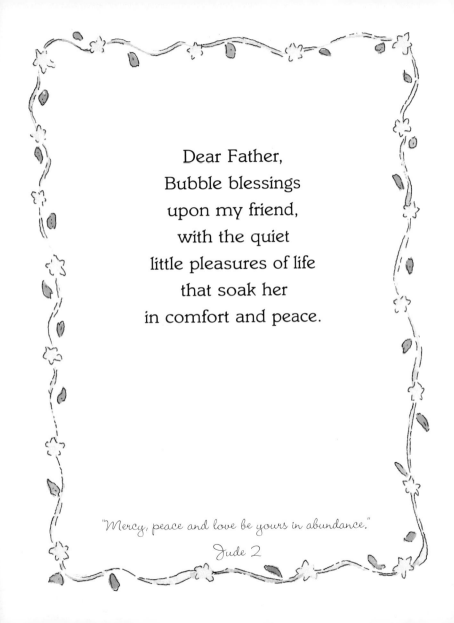

Dear Father,
Bubble blessings
upon my friend,
with the quiet
little pleasures of life
that soak her
in comfort and peace.

"Mercy, peace and love be yours in abundance."

Jude 2

Carolyn Blaylock

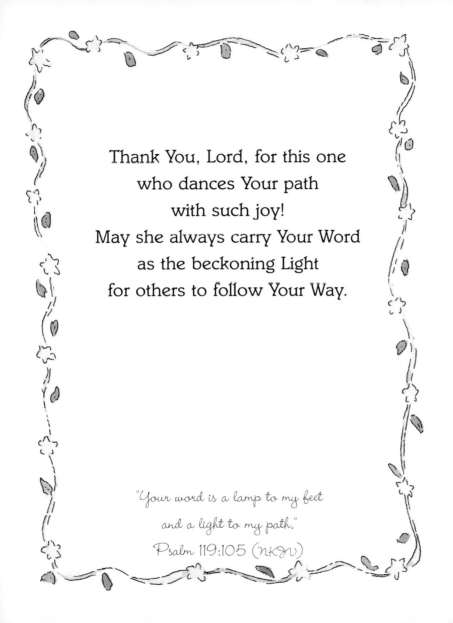

Thank You, Lord, for this one
who dances Your path
with such joy!
May she always carry Your Word
as the beckoning Light
for others to follow Your Way.

"Your word is a lamp to my feet
and a light to my path."
Psalm 119:105 (NKJV)

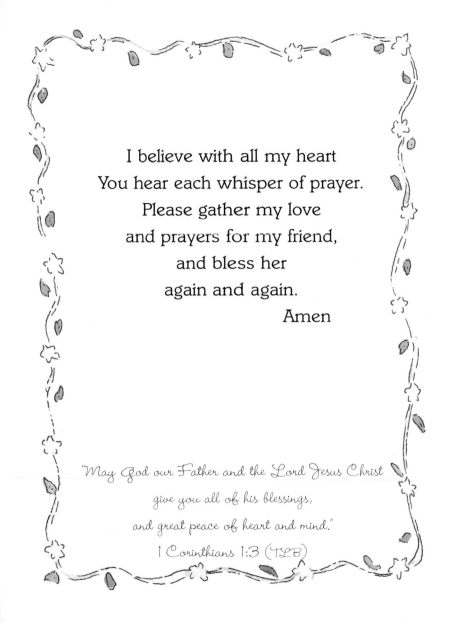

I believe with all my heart
You hear each whisper of prayer.
Please gather my love
and prayers for my friend,
and bless her
again and again.
Amen

"May God our Father and the Lord Jesus Christ

give you all of his blessings,

and great peace of heart and mind."

1 Corinthians 1:3 (TLB)